Published in 2020 by
**KidHaven Publishing, an Imprint of
Greenhaven Publishing, LLC**
353 3rd Avenue
Suite 255
New York, NY 10010

Edited by: Kirsty Holmes
Designed by: Amy Li

Cataloging-in-Publication Data

Names: Wood, John.
Title: Bacteria in our world / John Wood.
Description: New York : KidHaven Publishing, 2020. | Series:
Under the microscope | Includes glossary and index.
Identifiers: ISBN 9781534533134 (pbk.) | ISBN 9781534533158
(library bound) | ISBN 9781534533141 (6 pack) | ISBN
9781534533165 (ebook)
Subjects: LCSH: Bacteria--Juvenile literature.
Classification: LCC QR74.8 W663 2020 | DDC 579.3--dc23

Printed in the United States of America

CPSIA compliance information: Batch #BW20KL: For further information contact
Greenhaven Publishing LLC, New York, New York at 1-844-317-7404.

Please visit our website, www.greenhavenpublishing.com. For
a free color catalog of all our high-quality books, call toll free
1-844-317-7404 or fax 1-844-317-7405.

PHOTO CREDITS

CONTENTS

WORDS THAT LOOK LIKE THIS CAN BE FOUND IN THE GLOSSARY ON PAGE 24.

WHAT ARE BACTERIA?

Every living thing is made up of cells. Cells are like tiny building blocks. They are very small – in fact, they are too small to see.

HUMANS ARE MADE UP OF TRILLIONS OF CELLS.

THERE ARE
MORE BACTERIA CELLS
IN YOUR BODY THAN
HUMAN CELLS!

Bacteria (singular: bacterium) are living things that are
made up of one cell. Bacteria are found everywhere
in the world, from the bottom of the ocean to inside
your own body.

WHAT IS A MICROSCOPE?

Microscopes are used to see very small things that can't be seen with just our eyes. There is a whole world of living things that would be **invisible** to us without a microscope.

MICROSCOPE

Some microscopes are more powerful than others. **Scientists** use very powerful microscopes, like the one in the picture below.

IT IS TIME TO EXPLORE THE TINY WORLD OF BACTERIA. LET'S GO MEET SOME!

Some types of bacteria are harmful. This means people can get ill if too many bad bacteria get inside their body.

IT IS IMPORTANT TO WASH YOUR HANDS IN ORDER TO CLEAN THE BAD BACTERIA AWAY.

There are many everyday objects that have a lot more bacteria on them than you might think. Computer keyboards can have a huge amount of invisible bacteria on them.

MANY KEYBOARDS HAVE MORE HARMFUL BACTERIA ON THEM THAN TOILET SEATS DO!

LET'S TURN THE PAGE AND LOOK UNDER THE MICROSCOPE!

Bacteria are much smaller and simpler than the cells that make up animals and plants. The jellylike insides of the cell are usually protected by a cell wall on the outside.

EVEN THE BIGGEST BACTERIA ARE LESS THAN A MILLIMETER IN LENGTH.

The bacterium under the microscope on page 10 is rod-shaped. However, bacteria can come in all sorts of shapes. They are commonly shaped like balls, rods, or spirals.

ROD

BALL

SPIRAL

BACTERIA CAN CAUSE ILLNESSES SUCH AS PNEUMONIA (SAY: NEW-MOWN-YAH).

11

APPLE

Bacteria need four things to help them grow. They need warmth, water, time, and **nutrients**. Nutrients are found in living things and throughout nature.

WE KEEP THINGS IN THE FREEZER TO STOP BACTERIA FROM GROWING. THERE IS NOT ENOUGH WARMTH FOR BACTERIA TO GROW.

Food can be an especially nice place for bacteria to grow. For example, an apple contains lots of moisture and nutrients. In a warm enough room, the bacteria will grow quickly.

BACTERIA ABSORB WATER AND NUTRIENTS THROUGH THEIR CELL WALL.

LET'S TURN THE PAGE AND LOOK UNDER THE MICROSCOPE!

When bacteria have all the things that they need, they start to make more bacteria. A bacteria cell does this by splitting in two!

EACH BACTERIA CELL CAN SPLIT INTO TWO EVERY 20-30 MINUTES!

Many bacteria split in the middle. This creates two cells that are exactly the same. Sometimes the new cell grows from one end. This can create two cells that are slightly different from each other.

BACTERIA CELLS

INSIDE THE HUMAN BODY

Some bacteria live inside your body, in places such as the intestine (say: in-tess-tin). The intestine is a long tube in your body that is joined to your stomach.

THE INTESTINE ABSORBS NUTRIENTS FROM ALL THE FOOD YOU EAT!

The bacteria in your intestine help you break down food. These are called good bacteria. Without bacteria, humans wouldn't be able to survive.

HEALTHY PEOPLE HAVE LOTS OF DIFFERENT TYPES OF GOOD BACTERIA INSIDE THEM.

LET'S TURN THE PAGE AND LOOK UNDER THE MICROSCOPE!

This is E. coli. There is lots of E. coli found in the intestine. Most types are good, and are found in many animals, especially humans.

SCIENTISTS CAN USE DYES TO SHOW BACTERIA. SOME DYES GLOW IN THE DARK, LIKE THIS ONE.

Some types of E. coli can be bad when they are found outside of the intestine. A bad E. coli **infection** can make someone very sick.

BAD TYPES OF E. COLI ARE FOUND IN UNDERCOOKED BEEF AND DIRTY WATER.

DEEP IN THE OCEAN

Scientists think that some of the first living things on Earth were a type of bacteria. Over billions of years, some living things changed and became more **complex**.

EVERY ANIMAL AND PLANT CAME FROM SINGLE CELLS THAT WERE A BIT LIKE BACTERIA.

These early bacteria might have survived in hot areas at the bottom of the ocean. Bacteria and other animals can still be found down there now.

BACTERIA ARE VERY IMPORTANT TO THE WHOLE WORLD. LIFE WOULDN'T EXIST WITHOUT THEM!

LET'S TURN THE PAGE AND LOOK UNDER THE MICROSCOPE!

Billions of years ago, this type of bacteria changed Earth by creating more **oxygen** in the air. This is very important for life today – all animals need to breathe in oxygen to survive!

THERE ARE **FOSSILS** OF THIS TYPE OF BACTERIA THAT ARE 3.5 BILLION YEARS OLD!

Bacteria also help break down food and dead plants. This helps **recycle** what living things are made of so they can be used again.

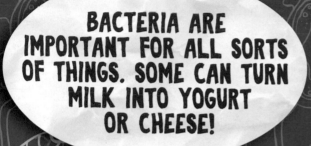

BACTERIA ARE IMPORTANT FOR ALL SORTS OF THINGS. SOME CAN TURN MILK INTO YOGURT OR CHEESE!

NOW YOU KNOW ALL ABOUT THE TINY, INVISIBLE WORLD OF BACTERIA. WHAT OTHER THINGS WOULD YOU LIKE TO SEE UNDER THE MICROSCOPE?

GLOSSARY

ABSORB   to take in or soak up

COMPLEX   made up of lots of parts that fit together in ways that are hard to understand

FOSSILS   what is left of very old plants and animals that lived a long time ago

INFECTION   an illness caused by dirt, germs, and bacteria getting into the body

INVISIBLE   cannot be seen

NUTRIENTS   natural substances that living things need to grow and stay healthy

OXYGEN   a natural gas that all living things need in order to survive

RECYCLE   to use something again to make something else

SCIENTISTS   people who study and know a lot about science

INDEX